Teaching My Heart

Fardowsa Ahmed

BookLeaf
Publishing
India | USA | UK

Presentation by *BookLeaf Publishing*

Web: www.bookleafpub.com

E-mail: info@bookleafpub.com

ISBN: 9789357445146

First edition 2021

DEDICATION

I dedicate this book to the One who gave me
my heart and returned it to me when I lost it.

ACKNOWLEDGEMENT

This book would not have occurred without the people and circumstances of my life–good and bad–that resulted in me wanting to write at this moment in time: thank you.

PREFACE

One of my favourite quotes is by Mevalana Jalaluddin Rumi: "Only from the heart, can you touch the sky." This quote has continued to inspire me, conjuring up images of the things that bring lightness to your heart, and cause you to surrender it to the sky. I have found, especially as I progress through young adulthood, that there is so much beauty and meaning to be in this quote- as of the feeling of your heart becoming light when you find joy, like a child. But also, in releasing the things that weigh our heart down when it becomes heavy, we teach our heart what does and does not serve us.

Teaching My Heart was inspired by this quote, and by the lessons I learned through my life experiences. I hope that you read it with your heart, and that you feel the joy of reconnecting with yourself.

Ocean Sand

ocean and sand
polar opposites

we meet in the middle:
you of water
and I of earth

mutually assured perfection
mutually assured destruction

Inconspicuous

Vengeance is not always loud
sometimes,
it is the quiet blaring sound
of footsteps no longer besides yours
doing what you never saw coming:
moving on

Perspective

It's okay to have different experiences of the
same person
But I will not emotionally orbit you
I will stay in my own orbit

Rose-colored Lenses

My life is starting to look grey
fading slowly,
chipped and dull around the edges
yet
lacking the mystique of an old black-and-white
photograph;
preserved memories cherished,
to which I compare

Restless with myself, I
look for a solution
could I maybe just—
no, that wouldn't work
yet—
what if I…
took out a newly dipped paint brush
and undid the grey entirely?

It takes some time before it dawns on me
that maybe there's something more to this
then all at once, I
put on my rose-colored glasses

and see this life with new eyes
because
it's not that my life actually is grey
but that it looks (italics for looks) grey
I've just been reliving my past
instead of facing my present

With glasses perched on my nose
and vision that's crystal clear
my world is now awash with soft, vibrant tones
it's time I retold this story in color
my past is no longer an excuse to escape
building all that lies in front of me

What You Do

6

When you call me my love,
Qalbi,
Ruhi,
My whole heart melts for you

Sweet Dreams

You slept so peacefully
with a morning glow resting on your face

dressed with the hint of a smile
I wonder if you dream of me

Cosmic Love

The cosmos is the place we met
far away from reality and expectations

Doe-eyed and flushed with love
you pulled me into your world
and I invited you into mine

Maybe that's why it feels like we
only ever exist in another dimension:
we never really made a world for ourselves
where it really matters:
here

Lifelong Friend

Anxiety is an old ~~friend~~
companion —
I have a long history with

No matter how much she causes
my mind to
race,
second guess,
doubt and
put off
I know that she is also
the engine behind my success,
committed to my purpose
in some ways
more than I am

I can't help but choose performance
even when I know it comes with paralysis

There are always strings attached
when your checkmate is made
By a play made my someone else

Gone Forever

Some days are just for allowing
quiet waves of grief
to wash over you
for all that you've lost
and all that has changed

But most importantly
for all the different,
younger versions of you
that you let go of

Not knowing
they'd be
gone forever
when they left you

Irreversible Knowledge

I have seen your soul, and
you have seen mine

So even though
we act like strangers now
we are still
so much more than that

Release

Remember not to let your sadness settle
so far into you

Surrender it instead to the trees:
patient and deeply rooted
they are the perfect stoics

After Hours

It's 3 am, I'm lying awake
because although you're not here
your words have a mind of their own

I

don't need a blanket,
I'm warmed by enveloping caresses

I

fall even deeper
as my neck is brushed with a kiss

I

am positive you sent this my way ...

My love,
you
steal my breath away
without even having to try

Open Book

How could you not know what you make me
feel
when my soul lights up in your presence
unable to mask its truest opinion of you,
never seeming to get the memo

My mind is more cautious, it
asks to take a second or two to
pause
no, it is not unsure—
it just wants to be sure

All the while
my heart unravels

Undone

You leave me with hope
like fragrance sequestered in the
shy blooms
of budding roses

... then undone all at once

Find Me

I want you to find me:
to discover parts of me
I've never shown to anyone else
parts of me that,
once touched by you,
will come to life.

I want you to find me
to uncover my affection
and steal my attention

because when you do,
it's all yours
because if you're worthy
I'm all yours- *What are you waiting for?*

Crowd

Love and desire aren't
always good company

Still,
at the sight of you
I inhale suddenly

Because you
ignite both
in me

Universal Truth

Sunrise is for observing poetry
in the unyielding laws of the universe:

Like the sun ascends gloriously to the sky
each day
taking no days off
and
mesmerizing the few who
gaze upwards to watch

So does my love for you
and that
is a *universal truth*

Hesitation

I wish you didn't
know how
much I love you
and instead
know how
little say in it I
have anymore

Remedy

Distance is the remedy

When broken promises become habitual
When saying *I love you* is no longer instinctual

And
you don't even
look at me
the same way

Endings

Endings are for people who can admit to them,
you say
I bite my lip
as I hold back the thought:
we both know we're over,
 and instead
ask you to kiss me

The bittersweet taste of fading love
intermingles with the hollow hope, and
urgency replaces passion

Our lips tell the truth
far more
than our tongues do

Freedom to Be

If she could be anything
she would be a city at night
shrouded in mist and blanketed by stars
at once, partly obscured from sight

At night, the mind stretches on
alacrity tempered with contemplation
silent and still
with myriad veins that branch off during the day
distilling into one cohesive thought

... this must be what meditation feels like

If she could be anything
she would be a city at night
only instead of being veiled by the dark
reeling as if held against a pike
you'd feel her heart warm, see it glisten on her
sleeve
free to be different from whom you believe
what someone who embodies the night
ought to be like